Telephone Skills for Professionals in Health Care:

Service Excellence on the Line

Wendy Leebov, Ed.D.

Leebov Golde Group

**Telephone Skills for Professionals in Health Care:
Service Excellence on the Line**

Current Version: Copyright 2012; Wendy Leebov

Original Version; Copyright © 1995 by Mosby Great Performance
Reprinted by iUniverese.com; 2003
No part of this book may be reproduced or transmitted in any form or by any means, graphic, electronic, or mechanical, including photocopying, recording, taping, or by any information storage or retrieval system, without the written permission of the publisher.

Requests to the Publisher for permission should be addressed to **Wendy Leebov**; 625 Casa Loma Blvd., Unit 1406; Boynton Beach FL 33435
Fax: 215-893-3524
Email: wleebov@quality-patient-experience.com;
Phone: 215-413-1969

Keywords: Patient experience, patient satisfaction, healthcare training, service excellence, service improvement, excellent service, service quality, patient-centered care, HCAHPS, healthcare quality, leadership development, management development

About the Author

Wendy Leebov, Ed.D is a passionate advocate for creating healing environments for patients, families, and the entire healthcare team for over thirty years, Wendy Leebov has helped hospitals and medical practices enhance the patient experience. Wendy is currently President and CEO of the Leebov Golde Group. Previously, she served as Vice President and change coach for the Albert Einstein Healthcare Network in Philadelphia. A communication fanatic, Wendy has written more than ten books for health care, as well as toolkits, guides, instructional manuals, slide shows, and articles. Wendy's most recent books:
- **Wendy Leebov's Essentials for Great Personal Leadership;** AHA Press, 2008

- **Wendy Leebov's Essentials for Great Patient Experiences;** AHA Press, 2008

Wendy received her Bachelor of Arts in Sociology/Anthropology from Oberlin College and her master's and doctorate from the Harvard Graduate School of Education.

All Rights Reserved © 2012 by Wendy Leebov

About this Book

Since you have probably been using the telephone since you learned to talk in early childhood, you have undoubtedly developed telephone habits—how you answer, how you say good-bye, whether you do other things while you are listening, how you find other people requested by the caller, and much more. In the world of work, these long established habits might or might not serve you well.

Great phone skills are important to your external customers:
- Patients, their families and friends.
- Referral sources such as physicians, social workers, clergy, and school counselors.
- The community.
- Insurance companies and other businesses.
- Vendors and suppliers.
- People with the wrong number.

The fact is, successful people recognize the power they have to handle the phone effectively. They consciously decide how to act on the phone and how to use it as a powerful tool that helps them to serve their customers and pursue their other personal and professional goals. How about you? Recognizing that we're in a world where there's a lot we can't control, why not consider ways you can become a telephone star?

This book is designed 10 help you take a fresh look at your telephone habits and identify ways to fine-tune them, so that, when you're on the phone, you not only gel the results, but you also leave the person on the other end of the line impressed—with a positive impression of you and your organization.

The skills presented here take into account your busy schedule as well as the special needs of your external and internal customers.

Throughout this book, you will find suggestions and self-help exercises. Try them out with co-workers, family, and friends. By practicing key telephone skills, making gradual improvements, and applying the skills described here, you will achieve greater comfort in your telephone contacts and, ultimately, more gratifying results.

OTHER TITLES IN THIS SERIES:

Assertiveness Skills
Customer Service
Job Satisfaction
Resolving Complaints
Stress Management
Working Together

Telephones in Health Care

Simply stated, telephones are everywhere—especially in a busy health care setting, where we can not escape the urgency of telephones ringing, voice mail lights flashing, and beepers beeping all around us.

As demanding as it can be, the telephone is an efficient, rapid, and cost-effective way to communicate. Without leaving home or work, patients, patients' families and friends, physicians, insurance companies, vendors, and co-workers in your own organization can call in order to:

- Make appointments and get information.
- Ask about a patient's condition and negotiate treatment.
- Discuss a referral.
- Ask for help.
- Identify the needs of your organization.
- Ensure the smooth operation of your organization's services.
- And do much, much more.

Phone Skills Are Especially Important in Health Care

Following consistent and professional telephone procedures in busy health care settings is not easy. Lean staffing, multiple demands, and heavy workloads make even answering the telephone in a timely fashion difficult, let alone answering it in a way that demonstrates patience and helpfulness to the caller. In addition, many of the people who call health care facilities are distressed. The public generally is not happy about having to interact with health care personnel because it usually means that someone is sick or, worried, traumatized by an emergency, waiting for laboratory results, or trying to get vital information about a loved one's or one's own very precious possession—health. Patients and their loved ones rely on us to offer compassion and consideration in our sensitive interactions with them. Given these callers' vulnerability, hearing a curt tone or waiting a long time on hold feels to them like an insult.

Our telephone communication skills are also challenged when we talk with co-workers and other departments. Health care organizations tend to be mystifyingly complex. Just finding the right person to provide a needed service or supply crucial information is not always easy. And when you find the wrong person and that person is feeling overworked, it's not surprising or uncommon that communication can break down between two people who know each other only as faceless voices. Everyone is trying to do a good job but feeling interrupted, harried, distracted, or overburdened.

In short, health care settings are demanding workplaces, and the telephone takes on pivotal importance as the center of vital communication. It's a lifeline. Because of the challenges of working in health care, whether in a doctor's office, HMO, hospital, outpatient center or nursing home, achieving excellence in handling the telephone does not happen by accident. It results from deliberate effort. If you want to be a professional on the telephone, take the time to step back and reflect on how you can improve your telephone effectiveness. Sharpen your techniques. Consciously decide how you can handle typical situations in the best way possible, and do not leave it to habit.

Benefits Abound

Improved telephone communication reaps enormous benefits for the organization, its customers, and you. Among the benefits of top-notch telephone skills are these:

- You create calm, comfortable, secure conditions for patients and their loved ones.
- You help physicians and other health care professionals maintain their productivity.
- You contribute to building a positive image of your organization in the community-an image of compassion, caring, and efficiency.
- You reduce the likelihood of dangerous or expensive problems and procedural mistakes.
- You foster harmonious relationships among departments and co-workers (your internal customers).
- You make possible quick responses to needs and emergencies, and, in health care, time is of the essence.
- You reduce your own levels of frustration and stress—the frustration and stress that result when callers are annoyed with what they believe to be inattention, discourtesy, and unnecessary hassles in telephone interactions.
- You use your own time wisely.
- You feel pride in your professionalism and ability to handle the variety of telephone interactions that are routine in complex health care environments.

CARE ENOUGH TO GIVE YOUR BEST

Sometimes people feel helped because we have provided exactly what they wanted—our service, an answer to a question, advice, directions. Sometimes people feel helped because we have listened to them with patience and concern when they were troubled, hurt, frustrated or anxious. And sometimes people feel helped—even if we were not of any direct help at all—because we have referred them to the right person.

When You're on the Phone, Your Organization Is on the Line

Whether you answer telephones and field inquiries as a primary responsibility in your job or take telephone calls only occasionally, your telephone manner says a lot about the caring, concern, and professionalism of you and your entire organization. In making a call or answering one, you represent not just yourself, but everyone you work with and for.

Why is a professional telephone manner important? For one thing, many people get their first impression of your organization via an initial telephone contact. Therefore, the telephone is a customer service tool, a public relations vehicle, and a primary channel through which a health care organization—its personality and its proficiency—becomes known to the community. Often, the telephone is your sole opportunity to convey information, answer questions, and set activities in motion. Using the telephone, then, is your prime opportunity to make the right impression—not only the right first impression, but also the right impression over and over again. Rate your current telephone skills by using the following telephone skills rating scale.

RATE YOUR TELEPHONE SKILLS		
On a scale from 1 to 4, where a 1 means "not at all skillful" and a 4 means "very skillful," rate yourself on each of the following skills. Also, think about why you feel this way about your skill in each area.		
TELEPHONE SKILL		RATING
1	Tone of voice	1 2 3 4
2	Determining caller needs	1 2 3 4

3	Explaining information	1	2	3	4
4	Greeting callers	1	2	3	4
5	Getting information	1	2	3	4
6	Handling stress	1	2	3	4
7	Solving problems	1	2	3	4
8	Listening	1	2	3	4
9	Putting callers on hold	1	2	3	4
10	Transferring calls	1	2	3	4
11	Keeping the right things confidential	1	2	3	4
12	Being assertive	1	2	3	4
13	Screening calls	1	2	3	4
14	Handling multiple calls	1	2	3	4
15	Handling angry callers	1	2	3	4
16	Ending a conversation	1	2	3	4
17	Handling interruptions	1	2	3	4
	TOTAL				

Scoring: Add your total points. If you scored 53 to 68, your skills are sharp, although you do have a few opportunities for fine-tuning. If you scored 36 to 52, your score reflects an average skill level. By sharpening your awareness of what professionals do, you can experience some dramatic improvements. If you scored 17 to 35, your skills are below par to the point where you probably create negative feelings on the part of callers. Attention to skill improvement will reap dramatic benefits in people's perception of your professionalism and service orientation, as well as in your effectiveness as an ambassador of goodwill for your organization.

Finally, look over your scores and list the skills that you consider your strengths and the skills that you need to sharpen.

_____
_____
_____

Listening to Yourself

Before you read on, test your voice and your telephone skills with a tape recorder. Listen to yourself as you answer the telephone, carry through conversations, and conclude an interaction. Use this technique of audiotaping yourself and listening to how you sound, what you say, and how you handle various situations to evaluate your progress as you continue through this book. You will be tape-recording only your side of the conversation, so you might want to take notes to remind yourself of the nature of the calls. Hold on to these tapes so that you can compare your improved skills with the way you used to sound— and celebrate your improved effectiveness.

Give yourself a checkup now and then. Make sure you're using the skills and pointers given here.

- How does your greeting sound?
- Does your voice make you sound energetic, pleasant, eager to help, concerned?
- Do you listen well?
- Do you think on your feet and resourcefully solve the caller's problems?
- Do you sound like someone you would like to talk to if you made a call?
- Do you sound calm and kind when handling a complaint?
- Do you leave the caller with a positive last impression?

If your voice sounds a little hollow, put more energy or strength behind it. If your voice is thin and reedy, try lowering it a step. You want the caller to feel that he or she is of primary importance, so you should focus on what you are hearing and talk directly into the mouthpiece.

Also use your tape recorder in practice sessions with a co-worker. Using role-playing, try out right ways and wrong ways of dealing with the different types of calls and the various personalities of callers. You can help each other understand the caller's point of view and even make up standard scripts or protocols to use for situations that come up frequently.

Making Friends with Your Phone

While most people spend huge amounts of time on the phone, many find phone communication at work intimidating or at least a little anxiety-provoking. In fact, a telephone can seem a little bit like a fortune cookie— you do not know what message you will get until you pick it up. That unpredictability in itself can be intimidating.

Also, as you know from experience, telephones have no respect for "busyness." No matter what you are doing, how busy you are, or how urgent your work, answering a ringing telephone becomes the most important activity of the moment.

Jangling phones can mean jangled nerves, but there are ways to overcome what many people experience as an aversion to hearing the telephone ring. You can become a telephone star—without being startled.

KNOW YOUR PHONE SYSTEM

The first step to telephone stardom is learning to understand your organization's telephone system. With so many different kinds of telephone systems and telephone support on the market today, it is easy to go from job to job and never meet up with the same system twice. Follow these suggestions for making friends with an unfamiliar system:

1. Find out about your organization's telephone system and resources. Is there a voice mail system and can you get a number? How can you get an instruction booklet, job aid, and/or training session so you can learn how to use the system's features? Do people have beepers and, if so, who has them and how do you access them? Is there a telephone directory? How do you find out about numbers that have changed? Are there organizational policies about how and when to use the various phone resources? Are there protocols for voice mail and in-person greetings, for putting people on hold, and time frame requirements for calling people back? Who do you call with questions about how to use various components of your organization's phone system?
2. Read the telephone, voice mail and beeper instruction booklets, policies, protocols, and job aids. Time invested in learning will pay off for you by making it easy to reach people and respond to callers effectively.
3. If you don't understand the instruction booklets and other written information, find a co-worker who is better acquainted with the system than you are and ask for instructions.
4. If you still don't quite understand the system, ask your supervisor to find out who inside or outside your organization can help you. Your organization's telecommunications office should be able to

answer your most difficult questions. Training sessions also may be provided periodically.
5. Practice using the system with co-workers before you make mistakes with outside callers.

Fumbling with the telephone while your caller fumes does not leave a professional impression. And the difference between putting the caller on hold and disconnecting the call entirely is often only a slip of the finger. Knowing your telephone system may seem elementary, but it is a first and necessary step in handling every call with success.

Using Your Telephone System Wisely

The telephone operators in your organization want to give you the best possible service. You can help them do this by following a few simple suggestions:

- Use the organization's telephone directory to look up extensions that aren't at your fingertips rather than calling the operator for assistance every time you need a number.
- Give outside callers your direct extension number. It saves time and confusion.
- Forward your calls to voice mail or to a knowledgeable colleague whenever your telephones are going to be left unattended for more than a few minutes. That way your telephones will not ring unanswered, and your callers will not have to resort to calling your main switchboard with complaints that your operators cannot possibly resolve.
- Transfer calls yourself whenever you can. It is a lot more efficient and courteous than shifting callers from extension to extension.
- Report telephone problems immediately. Otherwise your operators have no way of knowing when there's a problem.

VOICE MAIL EVERYWHERE!

Telecommunications have been changing dramatically and quickly, from telegrams and phones, to answering machines, to fax machines, to voice mail with automated attendants that direct calls mechanically to the area that can best meet the caller's need. If your organization has a voice mail system, you certainly can benefit from learning to use it. If your organization does not have such a system, you still need to learn how to use one, since many calls that you make will be answered by the voice mail system of another person or organization.

Voice mail can improve your productivity and help you manage your time and priorities, all while increasing, not decreasing, your responsiveness to your callers.

Get to Know Your Voice Mail System

If your organization has a robot-like voice that greets callers and invites them to select a specific number or leave a message, find out whether you can replace that impersonal voice with a real person's voice. These days, all systems allow you to record real people's voices on the outgoing message. If you have a voice mailbox yourself, you can certainly record your own outgoing message.

If you have your own voice mail number or box, design and record your own greeting. You can do so much better than the canned greeting provided by the system's vendor.

- Write down your greeting and edit it carefully to make sure it's informative, friendly and smooth, and that it encourages the caller to leave a detailed message for you. Figure out all the information the caller needs, being sure to include your name, department or title, and statement of fact about why you aren't answering in person. Are you out of town, in a meeting, in today but unavailable, or what? And include when or how often you'll listen to your messages. The caller might say or choose to do something different depending on when they think you'll get their message. If you check your messages frequently, reassure the caller that you do. And encourage the caller to leave a detailed message, so you can address their needs, prepare to call them back, or respond completely to their satisfaction with a voice mail message to their mailbox. And, if at all possible, provide a number they can call if they need or want to speak to a live human being (making sure that the live human being is not likely to put their phone on voice mail too). Given all of this, the caller is more likely to leave a meaningful message that will enable you to respond without reaching them personally or prepare you to reach them with everything you need at your fingertips.

An Informative and Friendly Voicemail Greeting
Hello, this is Sam Smith of the Training Department. I'm conducting a workshop right now. So, please leave a detailed message and I'll call you back, if you'd like, between 4 and 5 today. If you want to reach a person, not a machine, please call Training Associate Dana Starker at extension 7077. Thank you and have a great day.

- Then, record your message, making sure you put some humanity into it, so you don't sound like a robot or a depressed person.
- Listen to your recording, recording it over and over again until it sounds like you talking—as you would sound in a face-to-face conversation.
- Change your voice mail message often. The more specific and timely you are, the more people appreciate it (or more aptly, the less bothered they are by it). Ideal (but hard to maintain) are messages like "I'm in a meeting until noon and then I'll hear your message and call you before 1 pm." While it takes good time management, care, and a good memory to update messages like this often enough, your callers will appreciate you and your voice mail box, viewing you as even more responsive than you were when you only had a regular, old-fashioned phone at your disposal.
- Learn about and use your system's many features! You may be able to do many or all of the following:
  - Push one button to respond to a caller's message immediately, without knowing the caller's number—and then go on to hear your other messages. This is great because you don't have to write yourself a note or look up a number or try to recall later the content of the message you received.
  - Replay a message you want to hear again.
  - Save a message.
  - Save yourself from hearing a message you don't want to hear, by pushing a button that allows you to skip to the next message.
  - Pause a message—to give you time to write something down, cough or whatever.
  - Send a message to many people at once, using a "broadcast" message.

- Find out a person's voice mail number by spelling the person's name on your phone after pushing the "directory" number.
- Find out the time and date when a message was sent.
- And much, much more.

None of these features is difficult to learn. If you do not already have a job aid with easy-to-read instructions, call the person in your organization in charge of phone systems. Learn one feature a week, practicing it several times until it becomes second nature.

Reaching Someone Else's Voice Mail Box

When you reach someone's voice mailbox, consider yourself lucky. In your own voice, you can leave a detailed message. Since an estimated 70 percent of all business phone calls entail the relay of information only and require no response, if you leave a detailed message, you can accomplish a lot without ever reaching a live person. Even if you want a response, by leaving such information as the question you are asking and when you will be available to receive a return call, you are much more likely to get a helpful and timely response.

A Few Tips About Using Another Part y's Voice Mail System

- When you reach an automated attendant, you can bypass all of the attendant's sometimes lengthy instructions if you know the extension you're calling. Punch the choice you want and you're there.
- Plan your message in advance so that, if you get voice mail, you're ready and can leave the kind of substantial message that will advance your goals. And say it in a conversational tone and language. Talk like you regularly talk—with informal but professional language.
- Instead of feeling self-conscious about leaving your voice on the message you leave, just make sure you sound upbeat and friendly and tell them why you're calling, so they don't feel that you're trapping them unnecessarily into a game of telephone tag.
- Make sure your message includes any deadlines for receiving a return call and, if possible, when you'll be available if you need to talk with the person, not the machine.

If you feel resistant to voice mail, congratulate yourself for being stubborn, but move on. Voice mail can save you precious time and can improve your communication with others.

How skilled are you with your organization's phone system? WHAT DO YOU KNOW? WHAT DO YOU NEED TO FIND OUT?	
On the list below, check off those things you know how to do with each component of your organization's phone system. Then go on a scavenger hunt to fill the gaps, because every gap reflects an untapped opportunity you have to save time and become more efficient.	
	Yes!
ABOUT YOUR PHONE: CAN YOU…	
Transfer a call?	
Redial by pushing one button?	
Store frequently called numbers?	
Set up a conference call?	
Put a caller on hold?	
Buzz someone in your suite/area?	
If your phone is also a fax line, can you explain to callers/senders how to use each function?	
IF YOU HAVE VOICE MAIL: CAN YOU…	
Change your message easily?	
Reply immediately to an incoming message?	
Call others' voice mail directly when you don't want to speak to a live person?	
Use the directory to find out people's numbers?	
Skip to the end of a message?	
Replay a message?	
Save a message?	
Find out when the message was left for you?	
Transfer a message to another number?	
Add a message of your own to a message you're transferring?	
Send a "broadcast" message (to many people at once)?	
Listen to your messages from a remote location?	
IF YOU HAVE A BEEPER: CAN YOU…	
Quiet your beeper?	

Store a number?	
Look at a previous number?	
Change the battery?	
Remember to carry it with you?	
Remember to respond in a timely fashion?	
IF YOU HAVE AN ANSWERING MACHINE: CAN YOU...	
Listen in on an incoming call before answering?	
Change the tape (if there's a tape)?	
Easily change the outgoing message?	
Listen to messages from a remote location?	
Save some messages, while deleting others?	
Program your most frequently called numbers?	

EXTENDING TELEPHONE COURTESY TO CO-WORKERS

Now that you have refreshed your knowledge of how to implement effective customer service strategies by phone, be sure to use your skills in phone interchanges with your co-workers. Show them the same courtesy you extend to the public. Your co-workers expect and deserve the same level of respect and care.

Here are a few tips particularly important in telephone interactions with co-workers.

Co-workers (and other callers) like it when you:
- Identify your department and yourself.
- Take time to transfer a call.
- Take the trouble to look up a telephone number.
- Ask permission to put callers on hold.
- Check back with callers while they're on hold.
- Apologize for keeping callers waiting.
- Take extra time and effort to track down information.
- Say "please" and "thank you."
- Say "good-bye," and don't just hang up.
- Speak calmly and distinctly and don't sound hurried.

Co-workers (and other callers) do not like it when you:

- Call them "honey," "dear," "sweetie," or something else equally inappropriate.
- Don't bother to redirect their calls when they've reached the wrong department.
- Place them on hold before they've had a chance to say hello.
- Fail to identify yourself.
- Refuse to take a message.
- Chew gum or food in their ears.
- Pick up the telephone while you're still talking to someone nearby.
- Hang up without saying anything when you realize they've reached a wrong number.
- Leave them on hold indefinitely, without checking back.
- Mumble your name so that they can't understand it.
- Slam the telephone on the desk when they're waiting to be helped.
- Come across as short or abrupt.

> ### WHAT DO YOUR CO-WORKERS WANT?
>
> *Find out by asking! Interview the three co-workers you most often talk to on the phone. Ask them:*
> - **How do you like to be greeted on the phone?**
> - **What do you think about the way I come across over the phone?**
> - **(If you have voice mail) What do you think of my voice mail greeting? And what do you think of the messages I leave for you on voice mail?**
> - **If you had a magic wand, how would you improve my telephone and voice mail behavior?**

BEFORE YOU ANSWER

You probably know from firsthand experience what it feels like to make a telephone call only to reach somebody who sounds so harried that you almost feel apologetic for calling—or somebody who sounds like they are paying more attention to their computer than to you, as you listen to their keys continue to click. The telephone does not know what you are doing when it rings, and chances are the caller does not even want to know. The trick is to pick up the telephone and sound as though the call is the most important thing in your job that you have been waiting for this call and nothing else for days.

You need to learn to relax, or at least to sound relaxed—and to concentrate and focus before you even answer. Here are a few tips on getting your act together when the telephone rings:

- **Stop what you're doing.** Put down your pencil, pen, coffee cup, and papers.
- **Take a deep breath** and clear your mind of what you're doing. Collect yourself.
- **Stop** if you're in the middle of an office conversation.
- **Turn** your attention to the call before you pick up the telephone. You'll be better able to listen and you'll be able to handle the call more quickly as a result.

This little routine should take only a few seconds. In time it will become so automatic that you can pick up the telephone promptly— no later than on the second or third ring—and without hesitation deal attentively, clearly, and courteously with your caller.

Remind Yourself:
Right now, make yourself a creative job aid to remind you to ready yourself to give the next caller your undivided attention. For instance:
Stop what you're doing!
Take a deep breath!
Focus!

READY? GREET LIKE A PRO

What do you do? When the telephone rings, in the moment before you answer, you may have many things on your mind. Perhaps you were waiting for a particular call and you wonder whether this is it. Or perhaps you are involved in something requiring intense concentration and you would rather not be interrupted. No matter what your job, you are a customer service representative.

When they walk into a room, some people seem to say, "Here I am!" They want everyone's attention to focus on them. When other people walk into a room, they seem to say "There you are!" and they make you the center of attention. Instead of focusing on how important you are to them, make it understood that they are important to you.

For most patients and their loved ones, the person answering their initial telephone query represents their introduction to the hospital, department, nursing home, physician's office, or physician. The staff member who answers the telephone must convey an impression of competence, caring and professionalism if that introduction is to be a positive, effective one.

Here are just a few of the characteristics you are likely to find in people calling health care organizations:

- Patients, and the loved ones who represent them, are apt to be concerned and frightened about their symptoms. They rely on you to be reassuring and confident.
- Patients are apt to be nervous about seeing a physician or meeting an array of health care professionals who are all strangers to them. You can help by conveying sincere trust in the physician, the health care team, and the organization.
- Patients may be worried about how long they will have to wait for a procedure, answers to their questions, an appointment, or a meal. It helps when you're optimistic but honest in giving them estimated waiting times.
- Patients and their loved ones may be just plain scared. Take steps to lessen their fear without making light of their nervousness.

What Do YOUR Callers Feel?

Adopt the point of view of your most frequent callers.
What feelings are they likely to have?

_____
_____
_____

What thoughts or concerns run through their minds?

_____
_____
_____

Because of these thoughts and feelings, how do you want to behave when you receive their calls?

Your role as a customer service representative includes helping the caller feel at ease and confident in your organization. In that first telephone call, the impression you make on the caller is the impression your organization makes on the caller. Your responsibility in this is twofold: to help the customer courteously and to represent your organization with confidence and professionalism. To do this, it is important to be:

- Considerate
- Confident
- Caring
- Committed—to your customer and to your organization.

So get ready!

- Collect yourself. Before you even pick up the telephone, smile and take a deep breath. This will help you concentrate on the call at hand.
- Put down your work. Stop any office conversation you may be involved in, and turn your attention to the phone.
- Answer promptly, never later than four rings.
- Immediately identify whom the caller has reached. For example: "Sunshine Medical Center, Admissions, Gerry Caldor speaking. How may I help you?" Or, "Parkland Care Center, Pharmacy, Pat Cather speaking."
- Listen attentively to the caller. Concentrate on what he or she is saying. Take the time to determine the caller's needs. This will save you time later.
- If you have trouble understanding the caller, tactfully interrupt and say: "I'm having difficulty hearing you. Would you mind repeating that?" Or "I'm having difficulty understanding you. Would you mind repeating that slowly, since I want to make sure I understand you?"
- Be careful to speak clearly and distinctly. Avoid being too casual ("Who's this?") or too formal ("May I ask to whom I am speaking?"). Strive to sound professional without sounding cold and uncaring. For example: "May I ask who's calling?"

Answering the telephone is easier if you have your own "greeting ritual." Customer research has shown that callers want to know whom they have reached, including the organization and/or department and the person, by name. Some people feel awkward answering the telephone with their own name, but to the caller it indicates that a real person, not an anonymous voice is on the line. When you tell people your name, it's like saying: "I'm accountable to you. I want you to know how to find me if you want to talk to me again." It provides a personal touch that is important for customer satisfaction and a habit that you can perfect with very little practice. Also, it frequently works to your advantage. If callers know your name and you know theirs, they are more likely to treat you with respect. And, if they know yours, you are under a bit more helpful pressure to put on your best telephone manners. Consider too that the caller can tell your supervisor how helpful and courteous you were!

The elements of a great greeting include these:
- **A warm hello**. Express a positive attitude toward the caller immediately with a "Good morning," "Hello," or, "Thank you for calling Elkins Park Imaging."
- **The name of your organization and/or department**. Callers want to know that they've reached the place or party they intended to reach. By giving your organization or service's name immediately, they'll know (and you'll find out too) whether they've reached the right party. If you leave out this important bit of information, it might take many more questions and some confusion before it becomes clear that they have reached the wrong place.
- **Your name!** While many people prefer not giving their name, this is not professional. Customers really want to know who's helping them. They want to be able to call you by name and call you back if they have more questions. They also believe that employees who don't or won't identify themselves are doing this in order to hide from responsibility. If callers call you from outside your organization, both first and last name are important. First name only sounds too informal. Some people think that first name only is adequate for people who field calls from only internal callers. But, that's not really professional either. If you make 100 calls to almost any organization and analyze the responses of people who do identify themselves, you're likely to find that people with lower status jobs tend to use their first name only, while people

with higher status jobs use both their first and last names. The forces that led to this tradition are worth questioning. Is the secretary less of a whole person than the executive? To be thorough, and to command the respect you deserve for being the professional that you are, give your first and last name. There's no risk to it and callers definitely perceive it as professional.

- **A few words of encouragement.** Ending your greeting with words like "How may I help you?" encourages the caller to get right down to the business at hand, while again showing your willingness to address their needs.

Great Greetings: Examples

- "Hello, Surgi-Center, Helene Robinson. How may I help you?"
- "Good evening, Einstein Medical Center, Hospitality Desk, may I help you?"
- "Good morning, Turner Associates, Patient Billing. May I help you?"
- "Hello, Member Services, Sid Harkins. May I help you?"
- "Good morning, Admissions, Jane Wise, how may I help you?"
- "Thank you for calling Center Care. Susan Hyland. May I help you?

Test Your Greeting		
Give the following checklist to three of your most frequent callers. Ask them to fill it out the next five times they call you and give you the results.		
Caller's Name		
Your Name		
When I called, your greeting included these characteristics:		
	YES	NO
1. A warm hello		
2. Your name		

3. Your department, service or organization		
4. A few words of encouragement or a sincere-sounding offer to help		
5. Other observations of note?		

But Some Callers Are Impatient!

Are you thinking "But, be realistic—my customers won't wait through all that"? The greeting suggested above is the ideal, but some people in some settings find their callers impatient. Try out the Cadillac approach and see how your customers react. And ask some what they think about it. If many people cut you off or express impatience, shorten your greeting without sacrificing your professionalism. How? By perfecting the way you use your voice. Instead of "good morning" or another warm welcome, get that warm welcome in your tone of voice. Make your voice sound upbeat. Answer with energy and a smile. And consider eliminating the words of encouragement at the end. Instead, say your organization/department and your name, making your voice tone go up at the end, as if you're asking a question. If you keep your tone positive and energetic, and move it up at the end, it leaves callers with the feeling that you are asking them to tell you how you can help them. Try it. While this is not ideal, it works as an alternative for the high-pressure situation where callers, too, feel rushed.

Design a greeting ritual for yourself by following the simple steps outlined below. Make using your personal greeting a habit. Sure, sometimes you might want to answer a different way for variety. But if using the perfect greeting becomes a habit, you will be able to offer it automatically, even on those inevitable bad days.

> *You need to start with a great first impression, and also end with a good-bye that leaves a positive last impression.*

DESIGN YOUR GREETING
Go through these steps to create, test, and revise a personal greeting ritual.
1. Ask yourself what would be the ideal way for someone in your position to answer the telephone. What's the best, short way you can provide this information? Also, what's the best tone you could use? Write down your answer.
2. Now, try your greeting on a friend and ask for feedback. Could he or she understand what you were saying? Was your greeting too long or too short? Was your name complete and clear? Was the feeling you communicated friendly and attentive? Write down the gist of your friend's comments.
3. Next, revise your greeting to reflect the feedback you received, and write it down.
4. Finally, try out your "perfect greeting" on someone else and make sure you've got it down pat.
5. Write down your final ritual greeting and put it right at your phone, so you can follow it when you hear the phone ring—until it becomes habit.

WHAT'S TO BE DONE WITH WRONG NUMBERS?

In a large organization, it is not unusual to receive telephone calls that do not belong to you or to your department. If the caller is lost, be the one to help the caller find the right department. Too often, calls are shifted from department to department and extension to extension until the caller, in desperation, gives up and goes to a rival organization.

Never say to your caller "You've got the wrong office" and leave it at that. Rather, tell the caller which office he or she has reached and offer to transfer the call to the proper office. Always be sure to give the caller the correct number of the office he or she wants for future reference and in case the transfer is disconnected or the line is busy.

Poor handling of lost callers is a poor excuse for losing customers. So:

- Take the time to understand what the caller needs and to figure out whom he or she should actually be calling.
- If you do not have the correct extension at your fingertips, take the time to look up the number.
- If you think you know the answer but aren't sure, put the caller on hold and call the other number to find out whether it's right. If it's not, continue the process until you can locate the department or person the caller needs.

Remember, when you are on the telephone, your reputation and your organization's reputation are on the line!

A GOOD AND GLOWING GOOD-BYE

To make sure your callers remember you with positive regard, you need to not only start with a great first impression, but also end with a "good-bye" that leaves a positive last and lasting impression as well.

Some people let the conversation fizzle. They end with "OK," "bye," "uh huh," or nothing. The fact is, none of these sounds professional. Callers tend to feel dismissed and discounted. They think they were not important to you and worse, that you are glad to get rid of them. To end on a positive note, summarize what you are going to do, use the caller's name, and add on a few polite words, like "Thank you for calling. Good-bye" or "Have a good day [or weekend, or holiday]." When patients and families are calling about a visit, a procedure, results and the like, an even better option is: "I hope all goes well for you [your loved one]. Thank you for calling."

In addition, let the caller hang up first. That way, you will know that he or she is finished and you will not risk having the caller feel as though you cut the call short.

In short, sound happy to have served the caller.

Make Yourself a Job Aid

List the four most typical purposes people have when they call you. For each purpose, design a line that serves as an effective good-bye. Then write these on note cards and post them near your phone for easy use.

CALLER'S PURPOSE   **A GOOD GOOD-BYE LINE**

_____
_____
_____
_____
_____

Pinpointing the Caller's Needs

You can sound professional and express a positive attitude toward the caller with your words and voice when you greet the caller and when you sign off. But unfortunately, this is not enough. While some callers state their needs immediately in a clear way, many do not. So you need to figure out what the caller needs. This can be very challenging. Whether callers are good at expressing their needs or not, they expect you to meet their needs competently and quickly. And you cannot unless you understand what they want.

Figuring out what the caller wants requires skills, particularly in listening and questioning. These skills are reviewed in the steps that follow.

1. **Concentrate**. To help, get a pen or pencil and a clear piece of paper ready for message-taking. And take a couple of deep breaths, reminding you "OK, now I'm ready."
2. **Listen and learn with a clear and open mind**. Listen, listen, listen. Set aside any preconceived ideas or assumptions about why the caller is calling and hear them express their needs fully, without you interrupting. If you listen fully, without judging or preparing your response, you'll begin to learn why they're calling.
3. **Show that you're listening by giving feedback**. In face-to-face conversations, people give each other eye contact. They nod, raise their eyebrows, and give other visual signs that they're listening. You don't have that luxury when you're on the phone. Instead, you need to reassure the caller that you're listening by giving a variety of verbal signals, like "OK," "I understand," I see," and "Wait a moment while I make sure I got that right." You need to avoid saying the same thing over and over and especially in a

mechanical voice. Both make you sound bored and artificial.
4. **Take notes.** Make sure you write down the name (including the correct spelling) of the caller, his or her exact number, and the facts, whether it's a message, something you need to locate, or whatever. If the caller asks for someone else, always ask for and record the caller's name, organization, department, telephone number and, when possible, ask politely about the nature of the call (e.g., "Would you like me to note what you're calling about?") This information will help your co-worker to determine the most appropriate order for returning several calls and to prepare for them efficiently. Don't forget to initial the message to let your co-worker know who took the call in case there are any questions about the message later.
5. **Ask probing questions to get all relevant information.** Some callers say what they need fully and completely, without any prodding. Others need you to ask questions—to tell them what you need to know in order to help them.
6. **Check your notes with the caller.** To make sure your notes are accurate, and to reassure the caller that you've heard and absorbed what they said, tell the caller what he or she said in your own words, including every important detail. Ask the caller: "If you don't mind, I'd like to make sure I got that right. You said _____." Ask the caller to confirm or correct your rephrasing of his or her information.
7. **Follow through.** Meet as many needs as you can immediately. If the caller wants something and you can get it quickly, ask whether he or she would prefer to wait or have you call back with the results. If you need more time than that, predict when you'll be able to call back and ask if that's acceptable. If you need to involve others in the request, explain the process and how long it's likely to take. If the caller reached you by mistake when trying to reach someone else in your organization, don't say, "You've got the wrong department [or office]." Instead, tell the caller which office he or she has reached and offer to transfer the call to the proper office. Be sure to give the caller the correct number for future reference and for use in case the transfer is disconnected. For example: "I'm sorry. This is Radiology, and you want Physical Therapy. I'll be glad to transfer your call to Physical Therapy. In case we become disconnected, or you get a busy signal, that number is_____. Please hold while I transfer your call."

GOOD LISTENERS AREN'T BORN THAT WAY

Here are some more thoughts on the essential and powerful skill of listening. In the context of telephone interactions, listening is a lot more than passively absorbing whatever your caller says. Telephone interaction actually consists of two primary activities: talking and listening. Sometimes listening can be a lot more important—and take up more time—than talking.

Good listeners are not born; they are made. You can learn to be a good listener with a little practice and attention. Here are some tips to help you:

> **Listen with purpose.** Ask yourself what it is you want to find out and what it is you expect or want to hear. What might your caller say that would affect your preconceived ideas or plans?
> - **Listen for meaning.** People communicate to us on several levels at once. There are the words themselves, the implications of the words as indicated by tone of voice, and the emotions behind the words. In a person-to-person contact, you also have nonverbal cues such as posture, facial expressions, and gestures. But on the telephone, you must be attuned to what you are hearing. You must listen for what is not said but felt, as well as for what is actually said.
> - **Eliminate distractions.** Whenever possible, focus only on the call. You want to give your undivided attention to your caller, and you want the caller to sense that you are focused on the call and are not distracted.
> - **Don't jump in before you fully understand what the caller is saying.** Try not to talk over or out-talk your caller or to reply too quickly. However, clarifying the caller's points or questions by briefly restating them helps you make sure that you understood what was said. Then you can formulate your reply. Checking your understanding of what the caller said takes a little extra time, but with practice it becomes quick and natural.
> - **Be an active listener.** Involve yourself in the listening process. Be aware of your own listening barriers and guard against them. Take the time to be aware of your thoughts and reactions as distinct from the caller's. Check for understanding.

You can improve your listening skills with practice. Start today!

> People communicate to us on several levels at once. There are the words themselves, tone of voice, and the emotions behind the words.

LISTENING PRACTICE

Enlist the aid of a co-worker to help you practice good listening on the phone.

- Ask this person to pick a topic that's important to them…a topic with some emotion attached to it. Ask them to call you to discuss this topic.
- When they call, put on your best listening hat. Reflect back the content of their message. And reflect back the feelings you hear by saying something like "You sound upset…" or "You sound disappointed…"
- At the end of the call, ask the caller:
  - How well did I listen?
  - Did you feel that I understood what you were saying?
  - Did you feel that I understood your feelings?
  - Did I jump in with my own thoughts too soon?
  - How can I come across as a better listener?

PROBING WITH QUESTIONS

As mentioned earlier, most people who receive phone calls receive quite a variety. Some people call with straightforward requests, simple questions, and the desire to leave bits of information that require no response. Others call with angry demands, complaints, or the anxiety and desperation of emergencies.

For most of these calls, even these routine ones, it is essential to ask probing questions to learn everything you need to know in order to help. Yet, skillful questioning takes conscious work—and practice.

There are two main kinds of questions that help you figure out what the caller needs: closed- and open-ended. Closed-ended questions can be answered with a yes or no or a few select words.

They usually start with "is," "are," "can," "will," or "should." Open-ended questions cannot be answered with yes or no or other single words. They open up conversation. They usually begin with "how" or "what" and sometimes "why."

Closed-ended Questions
- Do you want to make an appointment?
- Can I take a message and give it to your mom when she wakes up?
- Do you understand the instructions?
- Is Monday a good day for you to come in?
- Will you be at home to receive a call at 5:00?
- Can you arrive by 10:00 am?
- Did your mother take her medication this morning?
- Do you have your insurance card number with you?
- Would you prefer to hold or would you rather I call you back?

Open-ended Questions
- What are your son's symptoms?
- How would you like to pay for that?
- Why do you want to see the doctor?
- What characteristics are you looking for in choosing a doctor?
- Why do you need the report so quickly?
- How satisfied are you with the way our team serves you?
- How can we help you more effectively?

"Eavesdrop" on the following two telephone conversations and note the variety of open-ended and closed-ended questions used to pinpoint the caller's needs.

Conversation #1: When a Caller Calls for an Appointment

Staff: Good morning. Pediatric Associates, Sally Bond. How may I help you? (open)

Caller: I want to make an appointment for my son.

Staff:	I can help. May I have your name and your son's name, please? (closed)
Caller:	This is Helen Schroeder and my son is Eric.
Staff:	Has Eric been seen by anyone here before? (closed)
Caller:	Yes.
Staff	Do you recall the name of that person? (closed)
Caller:	No, and I don't care who he sees as long as it's soon.
Staff:	Fine. Let me see who would be best to see Eric. What are Eric's symptoms? (open)
Caller:	His ears are killing him and he has a fever.
Staff:	When did the symptoms start? (closed)
Caller:	Four days ago and it's not getting better.
Staff:	I can imagine that you might feel concerned. I'm glad to say that Dr. Harris can see you at 10:30 this morning. Can you get here by then?"(closed)
Caller:	Yes, thank you.

Conversation #2: When Your Boss Calls to Request New Information

Manager:	Bill, this is Joan. I'd like a report to show to the board on your service's patient revenue.
Employee:	What's the purpose, so I can find just the right information? (open)
Manager:	They want to see if our service is meeting budget projections."
Employee:	Would it help to give them an expense report too, not just a revenue report? (closed)
Manager:	Good idea.
Employee:	You want the report to cover which time period? (closed)
Manager:	Since July first.
Employee:	Do you want to see the revenue broken down by month? (closed)
Manager:	Yes.
Employee:	How would you like me to format the report? (open)
Manager:	I don't care, as long as it's clear.
Employee:	What can you tell me about the level of detail you want? (open). I could show revenue for each procedure or procedures that cluster around a particular diagnosis, or revenue for our entire service. What would you like? (open)

Manager:	By procedure, please.
Employee:	What else might be helpful? (open)
Manager:	I can't think of anything.
Employee:	How about revenue generated by each physician? (closed)
Manager:	No, that's not necessary. I think that's all.
Employee:	So, my understanding is that you want revenue and expenses for each procedure, for each month starting last July, and that any format I choose will be all right. Is that correct? (closed)
Manager:	Yes.
Employee:	And my deadline for getting this to you? (closed)
Manager:	Tomorrow by 5:00 pm, so I can look it over and be ready for my 9:00 am meeting the next day.
Employee:	Got it.

MAKE YOURSELF JOB AIDS

If you are in a job in which you receive many calls of the same type each day, make yourself a protocol, or checklist, that helps you give and get every bit of important information you and the caller need. If you have a protocol, you are less likely to forget to ask or tell something, and you will not have to rely so much on your memory— making the call a bit less stressful.

Find Out:	Explain:
- Caller's name	- Confirmed date and time
- Caller's number	- Name of caregiver
- Patient's name	- Preparation needed
- New patient? If so, age, address, phone, etc	- What to bring (chart, insurance card, payment, etc.)
- Caregiver wanted?	- Travel (where we are, how to get here, where to park, cost)

▪ Reason for visit (routine, special, symptoms)?	
▪ Preferred date and time?	
▪ Insurance carrier? Number?	

For instance, the medical staff member in conversation # 1 would find it easy to have a checklist like this to use when people call for appointments.

Another questioning technique that helps the caller say more is the "mirror" technique. With the mirror technique, speaking in a questioning tone, you repeat the last word or the last few words the caller said. For instance, Lester, a patient, calls a medical practice after receiving a bill and reaches Susan, a member of the office staff. Lester says, "I read the bill and was furious!" Susan replies "Furious?" And Lester goes on to explain. Or, after talking with her distraught mother, Mrs. Cohen calls nursing home director Florence D'Amico. Mrs. Cohen says, "My mother is upset and she is not thriving at all!" Mrs. D'Amico says in a concerned tone "Upset and not thriving?" And Mrs. Cohen elaborates.

Regardless of which techniques you use, you need to persist in finding out more and more about the caller's concerns until you are completely clear about what they want. Only then can you do whatever is needed to satisfy them.

HANDLING STICKY SITUATIONS

Some difficult situations occur frequently in health care settings and deserve special mention. When handled poorly, these situations can damage your organization's reputation with the community. But handling them skillfully takes little more than common sense. Unfortunately, the most effective response often is not the first response that comes to mind. Here are some descriptions of special circumstances and sticky situations, and the special courtesies that can make your behavior impressive and satisfying to your customers.

Where Am I?

Once in a while, a patient or a visitor may be referred to your office by mistake. When you receive a misdirected telephone call, keep in mind that the caller may have been transferred to several other offices before reaching yours. This can be very annoying for the caller, and by the time he or she reaches you, the caller may be quite angry.

Do not pass the buck. Answer the caller's questions as best you can, and do whatever you can to help locate the correct office or department by looking up the proper telephone number in your directory. If necessary, tell the caller that you need to do some further checking but that you will call back with the appropriate number as soon as possible.

When you transfer the call, stay on the line to make sure that you have connected the person with the correct department. Your time, effort, and courtesy will reflect positively on both you and your organization.

Why Are There So Many People but So Little Time?

The telephones are ringing, and patients, physicians, or co-workers are waiting by your desk to talk with you. Whom do you handle first— the telephone caller or the person standing at your desk? You need to handle this tricky situation so that neither your callers nor the people waiting to see you feel slighted.

Answering the telephone promptly demands urgency. But when you are speaking with someone face-to-face and the telephone rings, finish your sentence before answering the telephone. Excuse yourself from the person at your desk, look apologetic, and say: "Excuse me a moment. I must take this call quickly."

When someone approaches your desk while you are talking on the telephone, finish your sentence on the telephone and then put the caller on hold, saying, "Would you mind holding one moment, please?"

You will need to use your best judgment to decide the relative priority of the conversations. If you elect to continue the in-person conversation, ask your caller whether he or she wants to remain on hold or have you call back later. Be sure to apologize for the inconvenience. If you elect to continue the telephone conversation and keep your in-person visitor waiting, apologize to the person waiting and finish the telephone call.

Juggling Calls and Callers

Answering telephones in a busy health care setting can often seem like a circus juggling act. Many people become alarmed—even confused — when more than one call comes in at a time. Some of us have jobs in which we can use an answering machine, answering service, or voice mail to delay the need to take the call until we can concentrate fully on it. But in many health care settings, it is a poor business practice to have a recorded message instead of a live human being greet the caller. For instance, sometimes family members call a hospital to find out how their loved one is doing. Or a parent calls a doctor to ask what to do about a child's spiking fever. Or a prospective patient calls to schedule an outpatient service. If you do not answer, the individual calls another health care provider and your organization loses that business. There are many, many health care services that need to be staffed with people who are immediately accessible over the phone.

With a high volume of calls, and the pressure to answer each one "live," the task requires a cool head, manual coordination, and a few points of telephone etiquette. Here are a few tips to help you juggle multiple telephone calls with poise:

- When putting someone on hold to answer another call, ask the caller's permission. For example: "Would you mind waiting a moment while I answer another call?" And if the caller is willing to wait, be sure to use the caller's name when you bring him or her back to your line to resume the conversation. For example: "Mr. Jones, thank you for waiting. You were saying that…"
- If you can't take care of the second call briefly, ask the caller whether he or she wants to wait on the line while you complete the first call or wait for you to call back later.
- If the second caller prefers to be called back, take the appropriate information and call back promptly.
- If the caller prefers to wait on hold until your first call is completed, be sure to check with the caller periodically and ask whether he or she wishes to continue waiting.

Being put on hold is often a sensitive, irritating issue for callers. Keep in mind their feelings and the very real fact that putting them on hold is an imposition. Be as apologetic, courteous, and quick about it as you can be.

This kind of telephone juggling act separates the beginners from the telephone etiquette professionals. Refer back to this information from time to time as you read through this book. In the meantime, take the mini-quiz on the next page.

MINI-QUIZ

Circle the best answer for each question and then look at the answer key that follows.

1. When you are rushed or under stress, which of the following do you tend to do?
   A. Keep it to yourself and handle people calmly.
   B. Apologize for your mood and hope they don't take it personally.
   C. Let it show. After all, no one's perfect.
2. How many times do you usually allow the telephone to ring before answering it?
   A. one or two rings
   B. three or four rings
   C. five or more rings
3. If a second call rings on your line and no one else is around to pick it up, which of the following do you do?
   A. Continue to let it ring.
   B. Say to the first caller, "Will you please excuse me? I must answer another call."
   C. Say to the first caller, "Hold on a minute."

Answers
1. *The best answer here is A. It demonstrates a professional demeanor. Answer B isn't a bad idea if you slip, but it's best not to let it happen in the first place. Answer C is the worst. Remember that the caller is innocent. Your ill will makes you and your organization look bad.*
2. *The best answer is A, of course, one or two rings. It is common courtesy. But sometimes answering on the first or second ring just is not possible. Most service organizations make it a rule that every*

telephone must be answered before the fourth ring even though this might occasionally require jumping through hoops. Answers B and C indicate poor telephone-answering practices. Remember that people become impatient when they have to wait. The longer you take to answer; the more impatient they become.
3. The correct answer is B. It shows courtesy and acknowledges the caller. The practice indicated by answer A is annoying, and no one likes to be kept waiting for an answer. Answer C is abrupt and would leave the caller confused and irritated.

What Can You Say to an Angry Caller?

Taking a call from someone who is angry or who has a complaint can be difficult and uncomfortable. But there are ways to calm an angry person over the telephone.

The most important thing that you can do is to listen without being defensive. Often, just having someone listen allows people to vent their frustration until they reach a point where they can listen, too, and move toward solving the problem. Let the person know that you will do everything you can to help correct the situation. Impress on the caller that you care.

Acknowledge the caller's anger, but remain calm yourself. Speak softly. Give the caller your name. That will tell the caller that there is a real person at the other end of the line. For example: "I can hear your frustration, Mr. Cole. My name is Harriet Smith, and I want to help you."
Take careful notes on the call. You are going to want to follow up on the problem promptly and call the person back with a progress report if you cannot address the problem right away.

If you decide to refer the person to a manager or an administrator, advise the manager or administrator that you are transferring a complaint call. But before you actually transfer the angry caller to someone else, make sure that the caller has recovered from his or her initial anger. Above all, do not become defensive and do not make promises you cannot keep!

Your Angry Callers

At your workplace, do you have angry callers? If so, what do they tend to be angry about? Getting appointments? Delays? Unfulfilled promises? List below the three situations most likely to make your callers angry. For each one, figure out words you can use to acknowledge the callers feelings and rebuild his or her confidence in your services.

ANGER-PROVOKING SITUATION	HELPFUL WORDS I CAN SAY
Example: Having to wait too long to get an appointment	"I can understand your frustration at having to wait. It's just that specialists like Dr. Marsh are few and far between. In the meantime, if the situation calls for more immediate attention, here's our emergency number."

Your Situation # 1

_____

_____

_____

_____

Your Situation # 2

_____

_____

_____

_____

Your Situation # 3

_____

_____

_____

_____

How to Say "No" with a "Yes"

Some callers want something they can not have—an appointment at a certain time, access to a particular caregiver, the cancellation of a bill, or an update on the medical condition of their loved one. Callers, whether patients, family members, physicians or co-workers, do not like to hear a "no" in response to their questions. It is challenging, but important, to find alternative ways to say no without starting a sentence with this off-putting word.

When the caller says "Is John Martin there?" and the answer is no, how about saying: "He's not available right now. I'll be glad to take a message, or perhaps I can help you?" Or: "He's out of the office right now. I expect him back at four. May I take a message?" If a person is requesting an appointment at 4:00 pm and there is no way you can provide that, how about saying: "I can offer you an appointment first thing tomorrow. Will that work?" If a family member reaches a medical clerk and asks about the medical condition of his or her loved one, how about saying: "Your father's nurse is up on that information. Let me have her call you." If a patient calls to complain about a bill, with the expectation that you will cancel it when you can not, how about saying: "What we can do is set up a long-term payment plan that will make payment much easier on you." Put the emphasis on what you can do, not on what you cannot.

What About Who Can Say What to Whom?

Confidentiality is one of the most important responsibilities of health care professionals. Every health care organization has policies and procedures that dictate the kinds of information that can and cannot be communicated over the telephone. Computer records, consent forms, who is getting which procedure, diagnoses, ability to pay, and much more all need to be treated with confidentiality. Typically, it is inappropriate for hospitals, HMOs, nursing homes and doctors' offices to give a patient's family, friends, or co-workers personal or health-related information about the patient over the telephone. What is their illness? What is the treatment? How are they faring? When will they be discharged? Who is with them at the moment? The answers to all of these questions are privileged information to be shared only with specific people clearly charged with providing care to the patient.

Confidentiality is also an issue among employees. It is inappropriate to share information about co-workers' personnel records, home addresses and telephone numbers, salaries, performance evaluations, health status, and similar topics unless handling such information is specifically built in to your job function. If your organization's rules about confidentiality are not clear to you, ask your supervisor to clarify them.

Who can tell what to whom is not the only confidentiality question. Breeches of confidentiality occur around telephones when people say appropriate things into the telephone so loudly that others can hear them. In addition, too often, confidential messages are left on desks and counters for anyone to read.

As hard as it is to resist sharing what might seem like good gossip or patient information that shows how well informed you are, the true professional resists this temptation. The professional takes pains to protect people's privacy and, as a result, to protect the trust people invest in his or her organization.

If you have noticed breeches of confidentiality owing to the nature of your telephone system, the location of your telephones, or people's behavior around your telephones, you would contribute to the well-being of patients and co-workers by sharing this observation with your supervisor. You will be a valued contributor to your organization if you take steps to improve the protection of confidential information—information that is private, personal, and precious in the eyes of its owner.

How Can You Tell People to Hold That Line?

Putting a caller on hold may be as easy as pushing a button, but to the caller it can be annoying and uncomfortable. Especially these days, people do not have a lot of time to wait on the telephone line. Also, many people interpret being put on hold as being momentarily abandoned. In any case, putting a caller on hold is a sensitive matter that requires tact and courtesy, and it should only be done for good reason. Here are a few reasons why you might have to put callers on hold:

- To consult with someone else in your office to find the information the caller needs.
- To retrieve patient charts or other documentation that you need to complete the call.
- To transfer the caller to another extension.
- To call another extension for information.
- To answer another incoming call.
- To handle an urgent matter that comes up in your office.

If you must move away from the telephone while the caller is on the line—for example, to find the information the caller needs—put the telephone on hold to block out background noise. When you leave the receiver on the desk with the line open, the background noise can be unnerving to the person waiting on the telephone, and the caller may come away with the impression that the organization lacks professionalism.

Never put callers on hold without first telling them that you are going to do so and asking their permission. You might say: "I need to put you on hold while I look that up. Is that all right?" You could also give callers the option of having you call them back: "I can put you on hold, or would you prefer that I call you back with the information?" Particularly when you know information retrieval will take more than a few seconds, give the caller a choice: "This may take a while. Would you mind staying on the line for a moment, or would you prefer that I call you back?"

Never keep a caller on hold for more than a minute without checking back to reassure him or her that you are still working on the question. Be sure to use the caller's name so that you both know you are talking with the right person. For example: "Mrs. Smith, this will take some more time. Do you wish to continue to hold, or should I call you back?"

What Should You Do with the Other Call on the Line?

Suppose that you are on the telephone with a caller and your other line rings. The second call is also important and must be answered after one or two rings. In such cases, ask your first caller, "Would you mind waiting a moment while I answer another line?" Then pick up the second call. If the first caller cannot wait on hold, ask for a number so that you can call back to complete the conversation.

If your first caller remains on hold, but the second call can not be taken care of briefly, ask the second caller to remain on hold while you complete the first conversation or offer to call him or her back. If the second caller chooses to remain on hold, check back periodically to assure him or her that you have not forgotten the call, and always ask whether the caller wishes to continue waiting.

Roleplay with your co-workers in various situations that require putting people on hold. If you have some free time, call each other on your office telephones and follow different scenarios. Think about times you have been put on hold, the reasons given for putting you on hold, and how you felt. Try to develop an attitude that will help your callers feel they are not being abandoned when you put them on hold. Use a tape recorder to hear for yourself the level of courtesy you can achieve with practice.

TAKING MESSAGES

Although telephone work consists primarily of talking and listening, it very often includes taking messages. Most messages are for people who are not available at the time the call comes in. Sometimes the messages will be to yourself, reminders of things you need to do to follow up on the telephone calls.

Before you take a message for someone else, you need to inform the caller that the person for whom the call was meant is not available. Here are a few pointers:

- It should be sufficient to say: "I'm sorry, he's not available right now" or "She's out of the office at the moment. I expect her back at 4:00. May I take a message?"
- If the person called is out of town or unavailable for a long period, ask the caller whether he or she would like to speak with someone else.
- If your co-worker has taken the afternoon off for personal business, it's really not a good idea to share that information with callers. "He's in conference" always comes in handy at such times. Take a message and be as helpful as you can.

- Avoid the following phrases:
  - "She's impossible to find or reach, but as soon as I can, I'll give her your message."
  - "She's working at home."
  - "She's always off somewhere. It's a real challenge to get her."
  - "He'll be back Monday. Would you like to try again then?"
  - "I'm sorry, but he's at the proctologist."

When you take a message, always write down the caller's name, organization, department, and telephone number or extension. Include any other identifying information, such as the name of the patient with whom the caller is associated. Don't be shy about asking the caller to spell out difficult names when necessary.

Record the date and time of the call, and try to record the subject of the call. This will help your co-worker decide the best order to follow when he or she makes return calls. Look for and locate any information your co-worker will need to prepare for making the return call. Be sure to put your initials at an appropriate place on the message so that your co-worker will know who took the call in case there are any questions.

Sometimes you may have to take a message for someone who is in and nearby but who is on the telephone or involved in some other work requiring immediate attention. You have a caller on the line, and you need to get your co-worker's attention in order to complete the call. To do this, place a written note in front of your co-worker explaining the situation. Be sure to wait for a response. Your co-workers will appreciate your courtesy and thoughtfulness as much as your customers will.

CREATE YOUR OWN MESSAGE FORMAT		
You can save time and thought by creating a format that helps you get complete information needed to produce a helpful, informative message. Here's an example of a message form developed for HMO and medical office staff:		
Patient name	**Date**	**Time**
Caller (if different)	**Adult?**	**Child?**
Phone (H)	**(W)**	

Referred by		
Regarding		
Purpose of appointment:		
■ Wants to see you because		
■ For second opinion because		
■ New symptoms		
■ Routine follow-up on		
■ Wonders if it's OK to		
■ Has questions about		
■ Wants referral for		
■ Other		
Insurance		
Remarks		
Appointment with		
Receptionist initials	Call date	

Now, considering the nature of the calls you get, design a message format that will make your message-taking more complete and efficient.

HANDLING TELEPHONE COMPLAINTS

Although health care organizations—and the people who work in them—try their best to provide the highest-quality health care services, complaints are inevitable. Nobody really likes to handle complaints, but someone has to, and that someone at least initially is often whoever answers the telephone. Here are a few tips that will help you handle complaints and help keep your organization's reputation intact at the same time:

- Encourage the speaker to express his or her complaint completely. Don't interrupt.
- Write down all important details, including short quoted phrases and important facts.
- Repeat these facts to the caller to make sure you have understood and recorded them accurately.
- Be sympathetic. It helps to calm the caller.
- Maintain a pleasant tone. Don't lose your cool!

- Tell the caller exactly what you intend to do with the complaint, to whose attention you will bring it, and when a response can be expected (if one is required).
- Apologize to the caller for the inconvenience or difficulty he or she has experienced, even if the problem was not your fault or the fault of the organization. This is an important gesture of goodwill toward the public.

Be sure to follow through. How complaints are handled is a strong factor in determining how the public feels about any organization. People tend to remember and to regard positively organizations that are responsive to their complaints. Complaint handling is a prime opportunity to develop and enhance good customer relations.

You can practice handling complaints and difficult calls with your co-workers. Use your tape recorder to review your responses and check the sound of your voice.

First, imagine what kinds of complaints might come through on your department's telephones. Take each one and roleplay the situation from the time the call comes in, through listening and responding to the complaint, to devising a satisfactory resolution.

In many work settings, certain complaints become more or less standard. Try to identify these routine calls and rehearse your handling of them with co-workers. Eventually, you should be able to make up all-purpose scripts for dealing with recurring complaint calls.

Remember to try to put yourself in the caller's position, and think how you would feel if you were faced with the same problem. Treat the caller with the same courtesy and concern that you would expect in a similar situation.

GIVE YOURSELF A CHECK-UP
After you have handled a complaint by telephone, reflect back on the call and ask yourself the following questions:
1. How patiently did I listen to the caller's complaint?
2. How well did I acknowledge the caller's point of view, frustration, or inconvenience?
3. Was I too quick to suggest a possible solution before I

heard all of the details?
4. After I fully understood the caller's complaint, did I offer helpful suggestions on solving the problem?
5. Did I reach resolution or closure instead of leaving the customer hanging?
6. Did I make sure the caller understood what I would do to follow up on the complaint?
7. Did I follow up as promised, in a timely fashion?
8. Did I sound genuine in my interaction with the caller?
9. How could I have been more effective?

DEALING WITH LANGUAGE DIFFERENCES

As our society becomes increasingly multicultural, most communities have people for whom English is a second language. That means that some staff and some customers have accents, and others may not be able to communicate effectively in English at all. Health care staff have a special responsibility to do whatever possible to understand and to be understood, and this includes speaking on the phone.

Here are a few tips for use when the person on the other end of the line is hard to understand:

- **Don't hesitate to admit that you're having a hard time understanding.** It does no good to complete the call without having understood the customer! Politely mention to the caller that you're having some difficulty understanding them. Tell them: "Would you please speak more slowly? I want to understand everything you say."
- **Don't raise your voice.** Some people act as if people who speak other languages are hard of hearing, and think that if they talk loud enough, they'll be understood. It doesn't work that way.
- **Take care to be polite.** Although you don't intend to be rude, it is somewhat rude to say such things as "What?" "Huh," "I don't understand you," and "What's that?" Watch your tone to make sure you don't sound exasperated. In a patient voice say "Would you please say that again, so I can help you?"
- **Give yourself time.** Don't hurry. Callers get agitated when you rush them. Listen carefully. Encourage them to take their time by

saying such things as: "I want to make sure I understand. Would you mind repeating that, please?"
- **Check that you've understood.** Repeat back key words. This will reassure the caller that you're listening and understanding.
- **Give them time.** Don't assume that a pause means they haven't understood you. The fact is, they have to work much harder to communicate than you do, and they need the time to do it. They are probably thinking in their native language and then translating it in their mind so that they can communicate in English with you. Don't repeat your words, as if they couldn't possibly have understand you the first time. Just give them time and repeat only if they ask you to.
- **Make job aids for yourself and keep them handy.** If you find that most callers who speak other languages speak the same other language, make yourself a list of key phrases and keep it near your phone. "Please," "thank you," "one moment please," "thank you for calling," "please wait while I get someone to help," "I want to help," "please repeat that," and "have I understood you?" are useful phrases. And don't worry about your pronunciation. Callers will appreciate your effort.

Some hospitals and health plans have organized interpreter services that provide over-the-phone and in-person interpreters when language differences impede important communication. In other organizations, people identify staff with various language capabilities and ask them informally to serve as interpreters—or just to help out—when a different language is needed. Find out about the resources in your organization, and use them. If you have people who can interpret, whether formally or informally, that is ideal. When you realize an interpreter is needed, you will just need to clarify which language, asking, "What language do you speak?" (If you're not sure), and then slowly say: "Please wait. I'm going to find an interpreter." Most people for whom English is a second language learn to understand these words. Then, connect an interpreter to the conversation, so you and your customer can understand each other.

Plan, Practice, and Sharpen Your Skills Telephone professionalism is not easy. There is a lot to it. Excellence on the phone takes planning, practice and the determination to be great not just good at it. You can increase your level of confidence and professionalism by preparing in advance how you will respond to a variety of telephone situations that occur almost daily. Write a brief script for each of the situations listed on the next page. Then practice your scripts with the help and advice of your co-workers. If you work out effective tactics for handling everyday telephone situations, you will have the best chance to achieve service excellence in telephone interactions.

When I answer the telephone:

On my outgoing voice mail message:

When I transfer a call:

When I return to a caller who's been on hold:

When I first hear a complaint:

When I realize the caller is irate

When I ask to take a message:

When I end the conversation:

When another line is ringing:

When someone asks for confidential information:

WHAT'S WRONG WITH THESE CONVERSATIONS?

Now that you have reviewed key facets of how a professional should handle the telephone, see whether you can apply what you know to improving the conversations on pages 53 and 54. In each of the two conversations, the health care employee's technique could be greatly improved to increase the caller's satisfaction with the telephone interaction. See whether you can diagnose the weaknesses in these conversations and then rewrite the scripts to increase the employee's telephone professionalism. Look at the following example before you go on to the two conversations to be revised:

(The phone rings.)
Ms. Adams: Hello, Admitting.
Receptionist: Hello, this is Dr. Harper's office. The doctor asked me to call to reserve a bed for a Mrs. Rebecca Martin for a hysterectomy. Do you have a bed available?
Ms. Adams: Yes. If you can get the patient here by 11:00 am, we'll take her tomorrow. We've had a cancellation.
Receptionist: Wait a minute. Dr. Harper doesn't want her to have surgery for two weeks because of his schedule.
Ms. Adams: In two weeks? I don't have that schedule right now. I'm going to have to look for it.
Receptionist: Wait. Can you call me back? I have another call to answer.
Ms. Adams: (Doesn't answer; puts receptionist on hold.)

In this conversation, Ms. Adams could have applied much more effective telephone tactics. Problems include the following:
1. Ms. Adams did not identify herself upon answering.
2. Ms. Adams did not give the caller time to explain her request fully. Neither did she ask probing questions to pinpoint what exactly the caller wanted.
3. When she did not have the right schedule, she explained this in a way that made her sound disorganized and inefficient.
4. Ms. Adams put the receptionist on hold abruptly, without asking permission and without reassuring the caller that she would be back.
5. If we were to replay this scene to reflect improved telephone tactics, it might sound something like this:

Ms. Adams: Hello, Admitting, Jean Adams.
Receptionist: Hello, this is Dr. Harper's office. The doctor asked me to call and reserve a bed for a Mrs. Rebecca Martin for a hysterectomy. Do you have a bed available?
Ms. Adams: May I ask who's calling, please?
Receptionist: This is Helen from Dr. Harper's office.

Ms. Adams:	Helen, you wanted to reserve a bed for Rebecca Martin. Did Dr. Harper say when he would like Mrs. Martin's surgery scheduled?
Receptionist:	In about two weeks, because of his schedule.
Ms. Adams:	I'll try to arrange that. Helen, I'd like a moment to locate the schedule for two weeks from now. May I call you back when I've located the schedule, or would you prefer to wait?
Receptionist:	Maybe you'd better call me back. I have another call to answer. My number is 555-6788.
Ms. Adams:	Fine. I'll call you back at 555-6788 within 10 minutes.
Receptionist:	Good. Thanks.
Ms. Adams:	Thank you for calling, Helen.

Practice Conversations

Read each conversation. Identify the problems in it and then rewrite the script using what you've learned about effective telephone tactics. After you're finished, you might want to compare your scripts with the revised scripts on pages 54 and 55. Since there are many possible improvements, not just one right answer, don't be too quick to criticize your revisions if they differ from those provided.

CONVERSATION #1

(The phone rings.)

Unit Secretary:	6 East, Ellen.
Dr. Fritz:	This is Dr. Fritz. My service said you called about Helen Bagley's medications.
Unit Secretary:	It wasn't me. Who called you?
Dr. Fritz:	There was no name, just your number.
Unit Secretary:	Well, Helen Bagley's nurse is on break, so I don't know who can help you. Why don't you call back in a half hour or so?
Dr. Fritz:	Can't you tell her to call me? This could be important!
Unit Secretary:	Everything is important, and I only have two hands, but I'll tell her to call you if she knows anything. What's your number?

Dr. Fritz: 555-6900, but I need to find out what this is all about, whether she knows anything or not.
Unit Secretary: Don't worry, somebody will get back to you.

CONVERSATION #2

(The phone rings.)
Mr. Marks: Environmental Services.
Mr. Foster: I'm calling my sister in 402. Is she back from surgery yet?
Mr. Marks: You've got the wrong number. You'll have to call Patient Information.

Revised Scripts

CONVERSATION #1

(The phone rings.)
Unit Secretary: 6 East, Ellen.
Dr. Fritz: This is Dr. Fritz. My service said you called about Helen Bagley's medications.
Unit Secretary: I personally didn't call but I'd be happy to check for you, Dr. Fritz. Would you mind holding for a minute or would you prefer that I call you back once I've found the person who can help you?
Dr. Fritz: I'll wait.
Unit Secretary: Thank you. Just a moment please. [Pause] Dr. Fritz? Thanks for waiting. I can't locate Mrs. Bagley's nurse; that's Margaret Smith and that's undoubtedly who called you. Will you give me a number where I can reach you? I'll

	call you back as soon as I can contact her, probably within a half hour.
Dr. Fritz:	OK, it's 555-6900, but make sure she calls me soon. This could be important.
Unit Secretary:	Yes, I'll be sure to have Margaret call you as soon as I can locate her, or I'll call you back myself. Thank you for your patience and thank you for calling.

CONVERSATION #2

(The phone rings.)

Mr. Marks:	Environmental Services, Manny Marks.
Mr. Foster:	I'm calling my sister in 402. Is she back from surgery yet?
Mr. Marks:	May I have your name, please?
Mr. Foster:	Brad Foster.
Mr. Marks:	Mr. Foster, I'm afraid you've reached the wrong department, but I'd be happy to find the right number for you. Would you mind holding?
Mr. Foster:	No. Thanks!
Mr. Marks:	One moment please. [Pause] Mr. Foster? Thanks for waiting. I don't know if your sister is back from surgery, but I can ring her room for you. In case no one answers, you might want to take down her direct line. Do you have a pencil?
Mr. Foster:	Yes.
Mr. Marks:	Her telephone number is 555-5124. Please hold while I ring her number for you. And Mr. Foster, I hope all goes well for your sister.
Mr. Foster:	Thanks.
Mr. Marks:	You're welcome. Now, just a moment please.

UNDERSTANDING THE 10 CRITICAL POINTS IN EFFECTIVE TELEPHONE COMMUNICATION

There are 10 critical points in handling telephone communications. Each point is essential to developing the ease, confidence, and competence required in effective telephone interactions. With practice, the points will become second nature and will make your work as a telephone professional more efficient, more effective, and more gratifying—for you as well as for your customers. Practice following these basic guidelines:

1. **Understand the caller's point of view:** Try to put yourself in the caller's shoes and imagine how you would feel if you were in the same situation. Develop an appreciation for the caller's problems.
2. **Let people tell their stories:** Draw the caller out with noncommittal remarks such as "uhhumm" or "I see how strongly you feel about that." Such remarks not only have a calming effect on the caller, they also help to reveal points of agreement important in finding a solution to the caller's problem.
3. **Listen:** Listening on the telephone does not mean sitting passively while the caller talks. Rather, you should listen with your mind, looking for paths that may lead to problem solving. Listening also means helping callers to communicate by asking apt and timely questions so that they can tell their stories fully. Listening is a skill that is not easy to master.
4. **Speak the customer's language:** Avoid using words and expressions familiar only to those who work in your organization or health care. Translate medical terms so that the customer can understand. Your purpose is to communicate, not to show off your knowledge. For example, "I made an appointment for you in P.T" or "Your brother is in I.C.U." may seem clear enough to you, but may not be clear to your caller. Take the time to explain exactly what you mean.
5. **Say it with respect:** Your telephone manner should show callers that you consider them worthy of respect and courtesy. Be sure to control the volume of your voice, choose words that are meaningful to your listener, and speak in a friendly, respectful tone.
6. **Make the caller feel important:** Sure, you speak to lots of customers in any working day, but each customer speaks with you only once. Make each customer feel important.
7. **Be prepared:** If you know in advance that someone is going to call you, perhaps for medical test results or to check on a patient or to receive an answer to a previous inquiry, review the appropriate file and materials before the call is likely to come in. Be current in your facts and resources.
8. **Be honest with yourself:** It may be OK to bluff in poker, but it's not okay in customer service. When you don't have the information

needed, don't fake it. Refer the caller to someone who does have the information. Or, better yet, offer to find the answer yourself and call back. Your customer will remember that you cared!

9. **Know how to stop an interaction:** When an interaction with a caller is allowed to drag on beyond resolution of the problem, it loses effectiveness. Once the problem has been resolved, you can courteously and tactfully end the contact. This should be done firmly but pleasantly. Often, saying "Thank you for calling" is all that is needed.

10. **Close the conversation cordially:** The way you close your telephone conversation should leave a cordial last—and lasting—impression. "Thank you for calling" leaves the caller feeling welcome to call again. Always let the caller hang up first. Otherwise, the caller may feel that he or she has been cut off.

IN CLOSING

Remember, the telephone is the communication lifeline between you and other health care professionals and between your organization and the people it serves in your community. As a professional, you are responsible for sharpening your telephone tactics so that this vital link between you, your customers, and your co-workers can be strong and effective.

Best-Selling Books by Wendy Leebov, Ed.D.

http://www.quality-patient-experience.com/wendy-leebov-books.html

Physician Entrepreneurs: The Quality Patient Experience -- Improve outcomes, boost quality scores, and increase revenue *(Book and CD-2008)* Built around the key areas in the CAHPS survey, this book and tool-packed CD offers quick and easy techniques that physicians and practice staff can use to enhance the patient experience—without sacrificing productivity.

Wendy Leebov's Essentials for Great Patient Experiences: No Nonsense Solutions with Gratifying Results *(2008)* Specific tools that enhance the patient experience and address the difficulties staff have in delivering the exemplary care they would like to provide. High-impact strategies for moving your service excellence and patient satisfaction to a new level, resulting in higher scores on HCAHPS and CG-CAHPS.

Wendy Leebov's Essentials for Great Personal Leadership: No Nonsense Solutions with Gratifying Results *(2008)* Valuable problem-solving and leadership development for health care executives, mid-level administrators, department heads, clinical leaders, and anyone who brings a passion to their work. Each chapter captures the essence of emotionally intelligent leadership and focuses on effective solutions.

Service Quality Improvement: The Customer Satisfaction Strategy for Health Care *(Leebov and Scott)* A goldmine of approaches for your service excellence initiative, that helps you build a service-oriented culture and focusing all employees on service excellence and continuous service improvement.

The Indispensable Health Care Manager: Success Strategies for a Changing Environment *(Leebov and Scott - 2003 Health Care Book of the Year)* Identifies ten role shifts needed by managers who want to add significant value to their organizations and enhance their employability. Self-assessments, case situations and concrete tools that build key leadership competencies.

Also by Wendy Leebov—practical guides that help frontline employees provide the exceptional patient and family experience

- Assertiveness Skills for Professionals in Health Care

- Customer Service for Professionals in Health Care

- Telephone Skills for Professionals in Health Care

- Resolving Complaints for Professionals in Health Care

- Working Together for Professionals in Health Care

Enrich Your Tools and Confidently Guide Your Team to the Next Level

http://www.quality-patient-experience.com/wendy-leebov-books.html